CHRISTMAS AT HOME

Old-Fashioned Holiday Recipes

HOLIDAY RECIPES & MORE

BARBOUR

P9-DCV-307

© 2009 by Barbour Publishing, Inc.

Compiled by MariLee Parrish.

ISBN 978-1-60260-506-0

Cover image left: Richard Eskite/Workbook Stock/Jupiter Images. Cover image right: Ann Stratton/Food Pix/Jupiter Images

Published by Barbour Publishing, Inc., P.O. Box 719, Uhrichsville, Ohio 44683, www.barbourbooks.com

Our mission is to publish and distribute inspirational products offering exceptional value and biblical encouragement to the masses.

Printed in the United States of America.

Contents

Here We Come a-Wassailing!

Here we come a-wassailing among the leaves so green;
Here we come a-wand'ring so fair to be seen.
Love and joy come to you, And to you your wassail, too;
And God bless you and send you a Happy New Year
And God send you a Happy New Year.

Wassail Bowl Recipe

2 teaspoons cinnamon
1 teaspoon ginger
2 teaspoons nutmeg
1 teaspoon cardamom
1 cup lemon juice

2 cups water
3 quarts sherry or cider
Sugar to sweeten
6 whole baked apples

Boil spices, lemon juice, and water for 5 minutes. Transfer to large double boiler, and add sherry or cider. Sweeten to taste with sugar. Put apples in the punch bowl while hot, and heat wassail just until hot. Pour over apples and serve. Makes 30 servings.

Apple Cider Nog

3 cups milk
2 eggs
¼ cup sugar
1 cup apple cider
¼ teaspoon salt

¼ teaspoon cinnamon
Dash nutmeg
Whipped cream
Extra nutmeg

Heat milk in a medium saucepan. Set aside. In a bowl, beat eggs and sugar until light and fluffy. Add apple cider, salt, cinnamon, and nutmeg. Whisk egg mixture into hot milk. Heat, stirring constantly until mixture simmers. Do not boil. Pour immediately into mugs. Top with whipped cream and a dash of nutmeg.

Holiday Pineapple Punch

1 quart water
2 cups sugar
2 cups pineapple juice
Juice of 6 lemons

3 pints chilled ginger ale
Red and green maraschino
cherries (optional)

Boil water and sugar for 20 minutes, then add pineapple and lemon juices. Stir and cool completely. Ginger ale should be added just before serving. As an added touch, freeze red and green maraschino cherries with water in ice cube trays.

Festive Pineapple-Grape Punch

1 cup sugar
2 cups water
1 pint grape juice
Juice of 2 oranges

Juice of 2 lemons
1 cup crushed pineapple
Crushed ice
Seedless grapes

Boil sugar and water for 1 minute. Chill, then add juices and pineapple. Pour into glasses partly filled with crushed ice, and add a few seedless grapes.

Christmas Cranberry Cocktail

2 cups cranberries
2 cups water

¼ cup sugar
2 cups pineapple juice

Cook cranberries in water until soft. Strain. Add sugar and bring to a boil. Chill.
Add pineapple juice just before serving.

Jake's Old-Fashioned Orange Cream

4 cups orange juice
  (not from concentrate)
3 cinnamon sticks

1 tablespoon vanilla
1 pint vanilla ice cream
Mini marshmallows

Combine orange juice, cinnamon sticks, and vanilla in a large saucepan over medium-high heat. Bring mixture to a boil, and reduce heat to low. Simmer uncovered for 10 minutes. Remove cinnamon sticks, and stir in ice cream. Cook over low heat, stirring constantly, until heated through. Do not allow mixture to boil. Serve with mini marshmallows.

Old-Timer's Eggnog

6 eggs, slightly beaten
4 cups whole milk
¼ cup sugar
¼ teaspoon salt

2 cups whipping cream or
    1 pint vanilla ice cream
Dash nutmeg
Peppermint sticks

In a large, heavy saucepan, mix eggs, milk, sugar, and salt. Cook and stir over medium heat until mixture coats a metal spoon. Remove from heat. Fold in whipping cream or ice cream. Pour into punch bowl or pitcher. Cover and refrigerate overnight. Sprinkle each serving with nutmeg. Serve with a peppermint stick.

Grandma's Hot Chocolate

2 ounces unsweetened chocolate
⅓ cup sugar
4 cups whole milk

Dash salt
½ teaspoon vanilla
Marshmallows or whipped
  cream

Place chocolate, sugar, milk, and salt in a medium saucepan over medium-low heat. Stirring constantly, heat until chocolate melts and mixture is well blended. Add vanilla and serve warm. Top with marshmallows or whipped cream.

For Starters

By remembering our kinship with all men; By well-wishing,
friendly speaking, and kindly doing; By cheering the downcast,
and adding sunshine to daylight; By welcoming strangers (poor shepherds
or wise men); By keeping the music of the Angels' Song in this home;
God help us every one to share the Blessing of Jesus,
In whose Name we keep Christmas.

HENRY VAN DYKE

Fresh Cranberry Relish

2 large oranges
4 cups fresh cranberries,
  washed and stemmed

2 red apples,
  cored but not pared
2 cups sugar

Peel oranges and reserve half of 1 peel. Chop oranges coarsely. Put cranberries, apples, and reserved peel through the coarse blade of a food chopper, or use a food processor. Add oranges and sugar; mix well. Refrigerate at least 2 hours before serving.

Spiced Cranberries

1½ cups water
4 cups fresh cranberries,
    washed and stemmed
5 whole cloves

2 tablespoons allspice
3 cinnamon sticks
3 cups sugar

Place water and cranberries into a medium saucepan. Tie spices in a small cheese-cloth bag, and add to saucepan. Cover and cook over medium heat, just until cranberries burst, about 10 minutes. Remove from heat; discard cheesecloth and spices. Stir in sugar, and cook 5 more minutes on low heat. Cool. Refrigerate at least 2 hours in a covered dish and serve cold.

Grandmother's Fruit Salad

6 bananas   6 mandarin oranges   ½ cup chopped walnuts
6 apples   ½ cup pineapple chunks

Cut all fruit in small pieces and mix together. Combine with nuts and dressing. Chill until ready to serve.

Dressing:
1 cup sugar   1 cup pineapple juice   1 tablespoon orange juice
2 egg yolks   1 tablespoon cornstarch   1 tablespoon lemon juice

Combine all ingredients, and cook in a medium saucepan over medium heat. Stir constantly until mixture thickens and is clear in color. Remove from heat and let cool. Store in refrigerator for several hours before adding to fruit.

Auntie's Bean Salad

1 (16 ounce) can green beans
1 (16 ounce) can wax beans
1 (16 ounce) can lima beans
1 (16 ounce) can chickpeas

½ cup chopped green pepper
½ cup chopped onion
¼ cup chopped pimento

Mix together and add dressing.

Dressing:

½ cup vegetable oil
½ cup white wine vinegar

½ cup sugar
2 teaspoons salt

½ teaspoon white pepper
¼ teaspoon black pepper

Blend dressing well, and pour over bean mixture. Toss. Marinate overnight in refrigerator. Serve cold.

Special Occasion Egg Salad

1 head lettuce
6 hard-boiled eggs, sliced
1 large sweet onion, sliced thin
1½ teaspoons salt
¼ teaspoon pepper
Dash paprika

¼ cup salad oil
2 tablespoons vinegar
1 teaspoon Worcestershire sauce
1 tablespoon minced parsley
¼ cup grated sharp cheddar
   cheese

Break lettuce into bite-sized pieces. Place lettuce in salad bowl; arrange eggs and onion in alternate layers over lettuce. Combine remaining ingredients and mix well. Pour over top of salad. Toss lightly.

Swedish Fruit Soup (Fruktsoppa)

¾ cup dried apricots
¾ cup dried prunes
6 cups cold water
1 cinnamon stick
2 lemons, sliced ¼ inch thick
3 tablespoons quick-cooking
    tapioca

1 cup sugar
2 tablespoons raisins
1 tablespoon dried currants
1 Granny Smith apple,
    peeled, cored, and sliced

In a large stainless steel pan, soak apricots and prunes in cold water for 30 minutes. Add cinnamon stick, lemons, tapioca, and sugar. Bring to a boil. Reduce heat and simmer covered for 15 to 20 minutes. Stir occasionally to prevent sticking. Add raisins, currants, and apple slices, and simmer until the apples are tender. Pour mixture into a bowl, and cool to room temperature. Remove cinnamon stick; serve at room temperature, or cover and place in refrigerator to serve later.

Noel's Jellied Salad

1 (20 ounce) can crushed pineapple
Several cups water
1 package lemon jelly powder
½ cup sugar

¼ teaspoon salt
2 tablespoons lemon juice
1 cup finely grated carrots
1 cup whipping cream

Drain pineapple and reserve juice. Set pineapple aside. Mix pineapple juice with enough water to make 1½ cups of liquid. Heat to a boil. Stir in jelly powder until it is dissolved. Mix in sugar, salt, and lemon juice. Remove from heat, and chill until slightly thickened. Add reserved pineapple and carrots. Whip cream until stiff, and fold into jelly mixture. Pour into jelly mold and chill overnight. Unmold by dipping into a shallow bowl of hot water and serve.

Kidney Bean Salad

⅓ cup mayonnaise
1 teaspoon prepared mustard
1 medium sweet onion,
  chopped fine
1 cup celery, chopped fine
1 small cucumber, diced
2 (16 ounce) cans red kidney
  beans, drained

4 hard-boiled eggs, cut into
  8 pieces each
Seasoned salt
Lettuce
Red and green vegetables

Mix mayonnaise, mustard, onion, celery, and cucumber. Fold in drained kidney beans and eggs. Season to taste with seasoned salt. Chill 2 hours until flavors are blended. Serve on lettuce, and garnish with red and green vegetables for Christmas.

Sweet Eggs & Beets

1 dozen whole hard-boiled eggs
1 pound whole cooked beets
1 medium onion, cut into rings

2 cups beet juice
1 cup cider vinegar
1 cup brown sugar

Place shelled eggs in bowl with drained beets and onions. Set aside. In a medium saucepan, bring beet juice to a boil. Reduce heat and add vinegar and brown sugar. Allow to simmer until brown sugar has dissolved. Pour over eggs, beets, and onions; cover and let stand in refrigerator for at least 2 days. Serve cold.

Farmhouse Potato Salad

4 cups hash browns
1 tablespoon salt in 1 quart
    boiling water
¼ cup sour cream
1 teaspoon salt
¼ teaspoon pepper
4 tablespoons diced
    sweet pickles

½ teaspoon mustard
¼ cup chopped celery
2 tablespoons sweet
    onions, chopped
2 hard-boiled eggs,
    shelled and chopped

Cook hash browns and 1 tablespoon salt in water, in a large covered saucepan, until tender. Drain. Set aside. Combine sour cream, 1 teaspoon salt, pepper, pickles, and mustard. Mix until smooth. Add celery, onions, and eggs. Stir lightly. Pour over warm potatoes. Toss lightly and cover. Refrigerate for several hours. Serve chilled.

Farmer's Holiday Soup

1 small sweet onion
½ cup celery
¼ cup butter
½ cup flour
8 cups chicken broth
4 cups shredded cabbage

¼ teaspoon white pepper
¼ teaspoon black pepper
12 ounces Polish sausage, halved
    and sliced in ½-inch pieces
2 teaspoons parsley

Sauté onion and celery in butter in a Dutch oven. Stir in flour until smooth. Stir in broth. Add cabbage and peppers, and cook until thick and bubbly. Simmer and add precooked Polish sausage. Top with parsley.

Country Chicken Corn Soup

1 (3½ pound) whole chicken,
    cut up
3 quarts water
2 stalks celery, chopped
1 large onion, sliced
1 tablespoon salt

1 teaspoon pepper
1 (5 ounce) package wide
    egg noodles
2½ cups whole kernel-corn
2 hard-boiled eggs, chopped
1 tablespoon parsley

Cover chicken with water in a large kettle. Add celery, onion, salt, and pepper. Bring to boil. Reduce heat and cover. Simmer for 2 hours. Remove chicken from broth. Separate meat from bone. Skin and chop meat. Strain broth and return chicken to broth. Bring to a boil. Add noodles and corn. Cook until noodles are tender. Add chopped egg and parsley.

Warm-the-Heart Chowder

1 cup cubed bacon
1 medium onion, chopped fine
4 tablespoons flour
2 cups whole milk
2 cups cubed raw potatoes

2 cups whole-kernel corn
2 cups water
1 teaspoon salt
½ teaspoon pepper

Fry bacon until crisp. Remove from pan and set aside. Fry onions in bacon fat until soft. Stir in flour. Slowly add milk, stirring until thick. Set aside. Cook potatoes and corn in water until potatoes are tender. Add onion gravy to potato mixture. Add bacon and seasonings. Serve hot.

Sausage & Apple Chowder

5 Italian sausage links,
   hot or mild
5 large potatoes, peeled and cubed
1 tablespoon dried oregano
1 tablespoon parsley
1 tablespoon basil
3 (15 ounce) cans chicken broth

2 tablespoons garlic powder
1 (15 ounce) can diced
   tomatoes
Water
2 (15 ounce) cans sweet corn
1 cup milk
3 small Red Delicious apples,
   cored and cubed

Over medium-high heat in a Dutch oven, brown sausage links. Drain off fat. Add potatoes, oregano, parsley, and basil. Toss to coat. Add chicken broth, garlic powder, tomatoes, and enough water to cover all ingredients in the pot. Bring to a boil, then reduce heat and simmer for 1 hour. Add corn and milk, and continue cooking over medium heat for 15 minutes. Add apples and cook until apples are tender but not mushy. Serve warm.

Christmas Cabbage Rolls

1 pound lean ground beef
1 pound ground veal
1 pound ground pork
2 eggs
1 cup milk
1 cup fine dry bread crumbs
2 teaspoons salt
2 teaspoons molasses
½ teaspoon ground ginger

½ teaspoon nutmeg
½ teaspoon allspice
1 medium onion, finely chopped
2 large heads cabbage
1 cup boiling water
Toothpicks
½ cup butter
1 cup whole milk
2 tablespoons cornstarch

Blend meats with egg, milk, and bread crumbs in mixing bowl. Stir in salt, molasses, ginger, nutmeg, allspice, and onion. Mix well. Cut out core of cabbages. Carefully separate outer 12 leaves of each cabbage, and reserve remainder for other uses or discard. Remove center thick vein of each leaf. Drop leaves into boiling water. Cover. Steam 3 minutes or until soft and bright green. Remove with slotted spoon, reserving liquid. Evenly divide meat among cabbage leaves. Fold sides in and roll up. Fasten with wooden pick.

Heat butter in frying pan. Brown cabbage rolls on all sides. Transfer them to a 3-quart casserole dish as they brown. Mix reserved water from boiled leaves with butter and drippings. Pour over filled rolls. Cover and bake at 375 degrees for 1 hour. Remove from oven. Drain off juices into measuring cup. Add milk to equal 2 cups of liquid. Stir in cornstarch. Bring to boiling. Cook until thickened. Pour over cabbage rolls. Bake uncovered at 375 degrees for 15 minutes or until browned and heated through.

Winter Potato Soup

1 small onion, chopped
2 tablespoons butter
4 medium red potatoes, diced
1½ quarts water
1 teaspoon salt

1 egg
½ cup flour
¼ cup milk
½ cup whipping cream

Brown onion and butter in saucepan. Add potatoes, water, and salt. Bring to boil, and cook until potatoes are soft. Make "rivels" by rubbing raw egg and flour together. Put in bowl, and then add milk. Cut through mixture with 2 forks. Drop "rivels" into boiling potatoes. Stir to prevent packing together. Cook 5 minutes with pan covered. Add cream. Serve warm.

The Trimmings

Today in the town of David a Savior has been
born to you; he is Christ the Lord.

LUKE 2:11 NIV

Stuffed Winter Squash

3 small acorn or butternut squash
1 large sweet onion, diced
1 tablespoon olive oil
1 cup finely diced celery
1 cup fresh spinach,
  coarsely chopped

1 cup whole wheat bread
  crumbs
¼ teaspoon salt
¼ cup finely ground almonds
2 tablespoons butter

Clean squash and cut each in half. Bake at 350 degrees for 35 minutes or until tender. Sauté onions in oil until soft. Add diced celery. Cover and simmer on medium heat until tender. Add spinach; stir to wilt. Combine bread crumbs with salt and ground nuts. Stuff squash halves with spinach mixture, and sprinkle the crumb mixture on top. Dot with butter. Return to oven for 10 to 15 minutes.

Turnip & Apple Puree

1 small yellow turnip,
  peeled and cubed
Water
1 medium apple, peeled, cored,
  and cut in chunks

¼ cup plain yogurt
1 tablespoon butter
Pinch nutmeg
Salt and pepper to taste

Cook turnip in water until nearly tender, about 15 minutes. Add apple and continue to cook until turnip is tender. Remove from heat and drain well. Puree turnip and apple in food processor until smooth. Transfer into saucepan. Add yogurt, butter, and seasonings to taste. Place on medium heat until heated through. Serve hot or cold.

Mary's Corn Pudding

1 pint fresh corn, with pulp
   scraped from cob
2 egg yolks
1½ tablespoons flour
1 cup whole milk

1 tablespoon sugar
1 tablespoon melted butter
½ teaspoon salt
Dash black pepper
2 egg whites, beaten to stiff
   peaks

Preheat oven to 350 degrees. In a large bowl, combine corn, egg yolks, flour, milk, sugar, butter, salt, and pepper. Mix well. Fold in egg whites. Turn into a buttered baking dish, and bake for 30 to 35 minutes or until set.

Cranberry Sauce

1 pound fresh cranberries   2 cups granulated sugar
2 cups water

Cook cranberries in water for 10 minutes, just until cranberries burst. Strain through a sieve, pressing pulp through with juice. Return to saucepan. Stir in sugar, and boil for 4 minutes. Pour into mold or small custard cups and refrigerate overnight. Unmold and serve with Christmas dinner.

Old-Fashioned Bread Stuffing

½ cup butter
1 cup chopped sweet onion
½ cup chopped celery, with leaves
8 cups bread cubes
2 tablespoons hot chicken
  or turkey broth

1 teaspoon salt
¼ teaspoon pepper
1 teaspoon sage
½ teaspoon thyme
½ teaspoon marjoram

Melt butter in a frying pan. Add onion and celery, and cook until soft but not browned. Combine butter mixture with bread cubes, broth, and seasonings. For a soft, moist dressing, use fresh or slightly stale bread. For a lighter, fluffier dressing, use dried, stale bread. Makes enough to stuff an 8- to 10-pound turkey.

Glorious Green Beans & Bacon

1 pound cut green beans
½ cup water
1 teaspoon salt
8 slices bacon

2 large potatoes, pared and
   cut into ½-inch pieces
1 small onion, sliced
3 tablespoons lard

Cook green beans in a small amount of boiling, salted water about 10 minutes or until just tender. Dice bacon and fry until crisp. Add potatoes, green beans, and remaining ingredients to bacon and lard; cook covered about 15 minutes or until potatoes are tender.

Grandma's Green Bean Casserole

½ stick butter
1 small onion
2 slices wheat toast, crumbled
6 slices bacon

1 quart green beans
1 teaspoon sage
½ cup sour cream

In a skillet, sauté butter and onion together. Add toast and let it absorb. In a separate skillet, brown bacon and then crumble it. Drain juice from green beans, and pour beans into baking dish. Add all ingredients to the green beans, mixing well. Bake for 30 minutes at 350 degrees.

Nana's Baked Beans

1 pound dry navy beans
6 cups cold water
1 teaspoon salt
12 slices bacon

½ cup brown sugar
¼ cup molasses
1 medium onion, chopped
2 teaspoons dry mustard

Rinse beans. Combine beans and water in a large saucepan or Dutch oven. Cover and bring to a boil. Boil 2 minutes. Remove from heat; let stand 1 hour or overnight. Add salt. Simmer partially covered 1 hour or until beans are tender. Drain, reserving liquid. Cut bacon into 1-inch pieces. Combine uncooked bacon, brown sugar, molasses, onion, and dry mustard with beans in Dutch oven or 2-quart bean pot. Add 1¾ cups reserved liquid. Bake uncovered at 300 degrees for 5 hours. Add additional water if necessary.

Willett's Broccoli-Rice Tradition

1 cup chopped onions
2 tablespoons butter
1 (10½ ounce) can cream of
  chicken or mushroom soup
1 teaspoon salt

½ teaspoon ground black
  pepper
3 cups cooked rice
1 (10 ounce) package frozen
  chopped broccoli, thawed
2 cups grated cheddar cheese

In a large skillet, cook onions in butter until tender crisp. Add soup, salt, and pepper. Mix all ingredients and put into buttered 2-quart baking dish. Mix well. Bake at 350 degrees for 35 minutes or until hot and bubbly.

Zucchini Casserole

2 large zucchini, cut in ¼-inch slices
2 celery stalks, chopped
1 medium onion, chopped
1 medium green pepper, chopped
1 cup fresh mushrooms, sliced
1 cup old-fashioned rolled oats
1 (16 ounce) can tomato sauce
2 teaspoons oregano

¼ teaspoon dried basil
½ teaspoon marjoram
½ teaspoon rosemary leaves
1 teaspoon dried red pepper
2 cloves garlic, crushed
Salt and pepper to taste
½ cup parmesan cheese

Prepare vegetables and layer in order listed in a medium casserole dish. Sprinkle vegetables with rolled oats. Set aside. In a medium bowl, mix tomato sauce and seasonings. Stir well and pour sauce over vegetable mixture. Sprinkle parmesan cheese over casserole. Bake uncovered in 350-degree oven for 45 minutes or until vegetables are tender.

Rudolph's Carrot Casserole

3 cups chopped carrots
Water
2 cups old-fashioned oats, uncooked

1 cup pecans, chopped
½ cup onions, chopped
½ cup butter

Cook carrots until just tender in enough water to cover and set aside. Sauté oats, pecans, and onions in butter for about 1 minute. Set aside. Then continue with sauce recipe that follows.

1 cup onions, chopped
½ cup butter
¼ teaspoon pepper
1 tablespoon flour

1 cup milk
3 cups shredded American
  or cheddar cheese
2 tablespoons parsley

Sauté onions in butter and pepper. Stir in flour until smooth. Add milk gradually. Cook, stirring constantly, until thickened. Add cheese, stirring, until melted. Remove from heat.

Mix previously cooked carrots and parsley in baking pan. Add sauce and stir to coat evenly. Sprinkle top with oatmeal topping. Bake at 375 degrees for 30 minutes.

Holiday Apple-Cranberry Casserole

4 cups peeled apples, chopped
2 cups cranberries
¾ cup sugar
1 stick butter
½ cup brown sugar

⅓ cup flour
1 cup old-fashioned
  oats, uncooked
½ cup chopped pecans
  or walnuts

Place apples and cranberries in a 9x13-inch greased casserole dish. Sprinkle with sugar. Do not mix. Melt butter in medium saucepan over low heat. Add brown sugar, flour, oats, and nuts. Pour over apples and cranberries. Bake at 350 degrees for about 1 hour. Serve with your holiday turkey.

Grandpa's Favorite Sausage Casserole

1 pound pork sausage
½ cup chopped onion
¼ cup chopped green pepper
¼ cup chopped celery
1 cup old-fashioned rice, uncooked
1 (10½ ounce) can cream
   of chicken soup

1 (10½ ounce) can chicken
   broth
1 small can mushrooms,
   juice and all
¼ cup chopped cashews

Brown sausage, remove from pan, and sauté onion, green pepper, and celery in drippings. Remove from heat. Add sausage and mix all ingredients together. Bake at 350 degrees for about 1 hour.

Sweet Potato Casserole

2 large sweet potatoes
3 eggs, beaten

¼ cup melted butter
⅔ cup evaporated milk

Topping:
1 cup chopped pecans
½ cup brown sugar

¼ cup flour
2 tablespoons melted butter

Wash, peel, and cut sweet potatoes. Boil for about 25 minutes, until tender. Drain well and mash. Stir in eggs, butter, and evaporated milk. Spoon into baking dish. Combine topping ingredients, and sprinkle evenly over sweet potatoes. Bake at 350 degrees for 40 minutes or until set.

Old-Fashioned Mashed Potatoes

8 medium potatoes, peeled and sliced
1 medium onion, finely chopped
Water
½ to ⅔ cup whole milk, divided
⅓ cup butter

1½ teaspoons grated
  parmesan cheese
1 teaspoon salt
¼ teaspoon sugar
Dash pepper

Cook potatoes and onion until tender in enough boiling water to cover. Drain and mash. Add ½ cup milk and remaining ingredients. Mix together. Add more milk, if needed, for desired consistency. Serve hot.

Corn Bread Dressing

3½ cups corn bread, crumbled
3½ cups biscuits, crumbled
½ cup melted butter
½ cup onion, minced
1 cup chopped celery

½ teaspoon pepper
2 eggs, slightly beaten
3 cups chicken or turkey broth
Savory seasoning to taste
Salt to taste

Place corn bread and biscuits in roasting pan. Add melted butter, onion, celery, pepper, beaten eggs, broth, savory seasoning, and salt. Mix together well, but gently, with hands. Place in shallow, greased 9x11-inch baking pan. Bake at 400 degrees for 15 to 25 minutes, uncovered.

Chestnut Stuffing

2 pounds chestnuts
1 cup chicken or turkey broth
2 tablespoons butter
¼ teaspoon sugar

Salt and pepper to taste
1 egg, beaten
½ cup fresh bread crumbs

Slit chestnuts and bake or roast for 20 minutes. Remove both skins, and place them in a pan with broth, using just enough broth to cover them. Continue cooking chestnuts until tender and almost dry, shaking occasionally to prevent burning. Rub through a fine sieve, and add butter, sugar, salt, and pepper. Mix egg and bread crumbs. Put all ingredients into buttered baking pan, and bake for 15 minutes at 350 degrees. Don't allow to get dry. Add more broth if necessary.

Granny's Corn Bread

2 tablespoons shortening
2 tablespoons butter
1 cup self-rising cornmeal
¾ cup self-rising flour

½ cup sugar
1 cup milk
1 egg
2 tablespoons oil

Put shortening and butter in a cool iron skillet. Put in oven at 425 degrees. Mix remaining ingredients in order listed. Pour in hot skillet from the oven. Bake 20 to 30 minutes until golden brown.

Squash Corn Bread

1 cup cooked winter squash
1 egg
2 teaspoons baking powder
1 teaspoon salt

1 cup vegetable oil
¾ cup yellow cornmeal
2 tablespoons butter

Mash squash. Beat egg lightly, and add to squash in a large bowl. Add remaining ingredients and mix lightly. Place the batter into a cast iron skillet or 9-inch square pan that has been coated with butter. Dot batter with butter, and bake at 350 degrees for 40 minutes.

The Feast

Over the river, and through the wood,
To Grandmother's house we go;
The horse knows the way to carry the sleigh
through the white and drifted snow.

LYDIA MARIA CHILD

Giblet Gravy

Giblets from turkey
2 celery stalks
2 bay leaves
1 small onion
3 garlic cloves
Salt

Pepper
All-purpose flour
1 cup broth
1 cup mushrooms, thinly sliced
½ teaspoon sage
Pan drippings

Simmer giblets (save liver for something other than gravy) with celery, bay leaves, onion, and garlic in a medium saucepan. Season with salt and pepper to taste. Simmer 5 minutes. Add flour to desired thickness. Add broth and mushrooms. Stir in sage. When turkey is done, add some of the pan drippings to this gravy, pouring off excess fat first.

Roast Turkey

1 (16 to 18 pound) turkey
Kosher salt
1 tablespoon dried rosemary, crumbled
2 teaspoons ground sage
2 teaspoons dried thyme, crumbled
1½ teaspoons salt
1 teaspoon pepper

1 stick butter, melted
Garlic powder
Paprika
1 (10½ ounce) can broth,
  for basting
Giblet Gravy (see p. 57)

Choose a plump turkey. Clean and dry thoroughly inside and out. Remove giblets and turkey neck from inside turkey, and rub liberally with kosher salt. Combine rosemary, sage, thyme, salt, and pepper in small bowl. Rub some in each cavity. If adding stuffing, pack body cavity loosely with the stuffing. If turkey is being stuffed, sew the opening closed. Tuck in wings, and fold tail in over stuffing. Brush top of turkey generously with melted butter, and sprinkle with garlic powder, salt and pepper, and paprika. Roast turkey, uncovered, at 375 degrees, basting frequently with melted butter and broth, or pan juices. After 1 hour, baste and sprinkle with seasonings again. Make a tent with aluminum foil, and cover breast loosely. Reduce heat to 325 degrees, and continue roasting for another hour, basting occasionally. Uncover breast and continue roasting 2 hours longer or until a thermometer inserted in the thickest portion of the thigh registers 165 degrees. When turkey is golden brown and done, allow it to sit for 20 minutes to rest before carving. Transfer turkey to a serving platter. Reserve pan drippings for gravy.

Holiday Stuffed Turkey

1 (14 to 16 pound) turkey
1 cup fresh mushrooms, chopped
2 cups cooked, chopped celery
1 cup chopped onion
½ cup butter

½ teaspoon dried savory
  leaves, crushed
1 (14 ounce) package herb-
  seasoned cube stuffing
1 cup cooked wild rice
1¾ cups chicken or turkey broth

Wash turkey under cold running water. Remove neck and giblets from inside turkey, and save for making giblet gravy. In a large saucepan, over medium heat, sauté mushrooms, celery, and onion in butter with savory leaves until tender. Remove from heat. Add stuffing, rice, and broth. Mix well. Spoon stuffing mixture into neck and body cavities lightly; do not compress. Sew opening closed with butcher's string. Tie legs together. Place turkey breast side up on a rack in a deep roasting pan. Roast, uncovered, at 325 degrees for 4 hours or until internal temperature reaches 180 degrees. Baste turkey occasionally with pan drippings and butter. When skin turns golden, cover loosely with tent of aluminum foil until done.

Country Holiday Ham

1 (7 pound) sugar-cured ham	2 cups maple pancake syrup
Whole cloves	½ cup cola

Preheat oven to 350 degrees. Remove skin from ham. Score the fat surface of ham with a knife in a diamond shape or any design, and stud with cloves. Pour syrup then cola over ham. Cover with foil, and bake for 3 to 4 hours, checking after 3 hours to make sure the ham isn't getting dry.

Holiday Ham Casserole

3 tablespoons butter
2 cups ham, cooked and cubed
1 (8½ ounce) can pineapple
  chunks, drained
1 (10½ ounce) can onion soup

3 tablespoons brown sugar
Salt and pepper to taste
1 (10½ ounce) can sweet
  potatoes, drained
½ cup chopped walnuts

In a large saucepan, heat butter and ham until lightly browned. Add pineapple chunks, onion soup, and 1 tablespoon brown sugar. Season with salt and pepper to taste. Bring to a boil, then remove from heat. Spoon into buttered casserole dish. Place sweet potato slices in an even layer over the ham and pineapple mixture. Combine walnuts and the remaining brown sugar. Spread this over the sweet potatoes. Bake for 30 minutes in a 400-degree oven. If you are serving ham on Christmas Eve, this is a great meal to use the leftovers for on Christmas Day!

Festive Holiday Ham

1 (7 pound) smoked ham
2 cups water
Olive oil
Whole cloves to cover ham
1 cup brown sugar
2 tablespoons flour
⅛ teaspoon garlic powder

⅛ teaspoon onion powder
⅛ teaspoon black pepper
1 (16 ounce) can sliced
  pineapple rings
1 jar maraschino cherries,
  cut into halves

Place ham in roaster with water. Cover and bake at 325 degrees for 3½ to 4½ hours. If the ham has an exposed bone, cover this with foil. Keep an eye on the ham as it cooks, and spray occasionally with olive oil during the first part of the cooking. Continue roasting until a thermometer inserted in center reads 160 degrees. Be sure thermometer is not touching bone. When ham is done, remove from oven. Lift off rind. Using a sharp knife, score fat surface crosswise, and dot with cloves. Set aside. Combine brown sugar and flour. Rub this mixture over the scored ham. Sprinkle lightly with garlic powder, onion powder, and black pepper. Place a pineapple slice on the ham so that one of the cloves will be in the center of the circle. Cover the clove with a maraschino cherry half. Each cherry half should be placed in the center of a pineapple slice. Continue until ham is covered decoratively with pineapple slices and cherries. Brown, uncovered, for 20 minutes in a 400-degree oven.

Traditional Roasted Goose

1 cup sauerkraut, cooked

1 apple, cored, peeled, and quartered

½ cup dry red wine, divided

1 (5 to 6 pound) goose

½ cup butter, melted

Salt

Pepper

In a saucepan, heat sauerkraut and apple. Put ¼ cup wine in roasting pan, and place in oven to heat. Stuff goose with kraut and apple. Rub goose with butter, salt, and pepper. Place in heated roasting pan. Place goose in preheated 500-degree oven, and baste every 7 minutes with remainder of butter and wine. Roast 35 to 40 minutes or until done. Place goose on Christmas platter and slice thin. Serve with pan juices ladled over goose and garnish with red apples.

Stuffed Cornish Hen

1 (6 ounce) package wild rice mix
½ cup diced celery
1 (5 ounce) can water chestnuts, sliced
½ cup mushrooms, chopped

¼ cup butter, melted
1 tablespoon soy sauce
Salt
4 (1 pound) Cornish game
  hens

Cook rice, using package directions; cool. Add celery, water chestnuts, mushrooms, butter, and soy sauce. Toss lightly to mix. Salt inside of birds; stuff with mixture and truss. Cook in preheated 450-degree oven for 15 minutes; reduce heat to 375 degrees, and cook for 30 additional minutes or until juices run clear.

Traditional Cornish Hen

4 (1 pound) Cornish game hens
Lemon juice
Garlic cloves, crushed
½ teaspoon garlic salt
¼ teaspoon white pepper

½ teaspoon sage
½ teaspoon thyme
½ teaspoon onion powder
1 cup chicken broth

Clean hens with lemon juice and pat dry. Rub with crushed garlic cloves. Season hens inside and out with mixture of remaining seasonings. Place hens in roasting pan; add chicken broth. Cook in preheated 450-degree oven for 15 minutes; reduce heat to 375 degrees, and cook for 30 additional minutes or until juices run clear.

New Year's Casserole

2 pounds sausage
2 cups sauerkraut

1 large sweet onion,
   cut into rings
5 potatoes, sliced thin

Put in baking dish in layers, starting with sausage then sauerkraut, onion rings, and potatoes. Cover and bake at 375 degrees for 1½ hours or until potatoes are done. Uncover and brown for the last 15 minutes.

Sweet Delights

"Where is the one who has been born king of the Jews?
We saw his star in the east and have come to worship him."

MATTHEW 2:2 NIV

Pumpkin Pie

2 cups pumpkin
¾ cup firmly packed light
  brown sugar
2 eggs, well beaten
1½ tablespoons melted butter
1 tablespoon molasses

½ teaspoon salt
½ teaspoon cinnamon
½ teaspoon ground nutmeg
¾ cup evaporated milk
1 (9 inch) unbaked pie shell

Combine ingredients; pour into pie shell. Bake in 450-degree oven for 10 minutes. Reduce heat quickly by leaving door open for a few minutes. Continue baking at 325 degrees about 45 minutes or until a knife comes out clean after inserting into the center.

Squash Pie

½ cup white sugar
½ cup brown sugar
½ teaspoon ground cinnamon
¼ teaspoon ground nutmeg
1½ cups squash,
   cooked and mashed

½ teaspoon salt
2 eggs
1½ cups whole milk
1 (9 inch) unbaked pie shell

Combine ingredients; pour into pie shell. Bake in 450-degree oven for 10 minutes. Reduce heat quickly by leaving door open for a few minutes. Continue baking at 325 degrees about 45 minutes or until a knife comes out clean after inserting into the center.

Granny Smith Apple Cake

1 cup vegetable oil
2 eggs
2 cups sugar
2½ cups flour
1 teaspoon soda
1 teaspoon salt

1 teaspoon cinnamon
1 teaspoon baking powder
1 cup chopped walnuts
3 cups Granny Smith
   apples, chopped
¾ cup butterscotch chips

In large bowl, mix oil, eggs, and sugar. In separate bowl, sift together flour, soda, salt, cinnamon, and baking powder. Add to egg mixture. Stir in nuts and chopped apples. Mix well. Spread mixture in greased 9x13-inch pan. Sprinkle butterscotch chips on top of cake. Bake at 350 degrees for 55 to 65 minutes. Cool and cut into squares. Bake one day before serving for best flavor.

Jam Cake

1 cup butter
2 cups sugar
4 eggs
1 cup strawberry freezer jam
1 teaspoon baking soda

1 cup buttermilk
3 cups flour
½ teaspoon cinnamon
1 cup nuts
Vanilla icing

Cream butter and sugar until fluffy. Add unbeaten eggs, one at a time, beating well after each egg is added. Add jam and mix well. Stir soda into milk. Add milk and flour alternately. Stir in cinnamon. Fold in nuts. Bake in 2 greased and floured 9-inch pans at 350 degrees for 30 to 40 minutes. Cool. Spread with vanilla icing and serve.

Cream Cheese Frosting

1 (8 ounce) package cream cheese, softened
1 teaspoon vanilla extract
1 cup powdered sugar
1 small container frozen whipped topping, thawed

In a large bowl, beat cream cheese and vanilla. Gradually add powdered sugar. Fold in whipped topping.

Amazing Carrot Cake

3 cups all-purpose flour
1 cup sugar
1 tablespoon ground cinnamon
2 teaspoons baking soda
1 teaspoon baking powder
1 teaspoon salt
¼ teaspoon ground ginger
1¼ cups unsweetened
   chunky applesauce

1¼ cups vegetable oil
1 cup packed light brown sugar
1 tablespoon vanilla extract
4 large eggs
2 cups shredded carrots (about
   4 medium-sized carrots)
1 cup walnuts, finely ground
⅓ cup red currant jelly
Cream Cheese Frosting (see
   p. 75)

Preheat oven to 350 degrees. Grease 9x11-inch baking pan. In a large bowl, mix flour, sugar, cinnamon, baking soda, baking powder, salt, and ginger. In a medium bowl, whisk applesauce, oil, brown sugar, vanilla, and eggs until smooth. Stir applesauce mixture, shredded carrots, and walnuts into flour mixture just until flour is moistened. Pour batter into pan. Bake 65 to 70 minutes until toothpick inserted in center of cake comes out clean, covering top of cake with foil if it browns too quickly. Cool cake in pan on wire rack 10 minutes; remove from pan, and cool completely on rack. When cake is cool, heat currant jelly until melted and smooth in a small saucepan. Brush melted jelly over top and side of cake to glaze. Spoon Cream Cheese Frosting over the glaze and smooth. Refrigerate cake if not serving right away.

Tapioca Pudding for the Holidays

3 heaping tablespoons large
   round tapioca
¾ cup water
4 cups milk
3 eggs, separated
1 cup sugar

1 teaspoon salt
1 teaspoon vanilla
¼ cup sugar
Pinch salt
Red and green sugars

In a covered dish, soak tapioca in water overnight. In the morning, add tapioca to milk, and cook in a heavy kettle very slowly over low heat until tapioca is clear. Beat egg yolks with 1 cup of sugar and 1 teaspoon of salt. Slowly add to milk mixture. Cook a little longer, and then add vanilla. Pour into a large casserole dish. Whip egg whites until stiff. Add ¼ cup sugar and pinch of salt. Place meringue over pudding, and brown in a 300-degree oven. Cook slowly until done, but check often to prevent burning. Sprinkle with red and green sugars.

Granny's Sugar Cream Pie

¾ cup granulated sugar
4 tablespoons flour
2 cups half-and-half
Dash salt

1 (9 inch) unbaked pie shell
1 tablespoon butter
Dash nutmeg

Mix sugar, flour, half-and-half, and salt in pie shell, using fingertips. Add more flour if it looks soupy. Dot with butter, and sprinkle with nutmeg. Bake at 350 degrees for 45 to 60 minutes. Pie will thicken as it cools.

Jelly Roll

3 eggs
1 cup sugar
⅓ cup water
1 teaspoon vanilla
¾ cup flour

1 teaspoon baking powder
¼ teaspoon salt
Powdered sugar
¾ cup raspberry jam or
    preserves

Heat oven to 375 degrees. Line jelly roll pan with aluminum foil. In small bowl, beat eggs about 5 minutes until very thick. Pour eggs into a larger mixing bowl; gradually add sugar. Blend in water and vanilla on low. Gradually add flour, baking powder, and salt. Beat until batter is smooth. Pour into pan, spreading batter into corners. Bake 12 to 15 minutes. Loosen cake from edges, invert on towel, and sprinkle with powdered sugar. Carefully remove foil; trim off any hard edges if needed. While hot, roll cake and towel from narrow end. Cool on wire rack. Unroll cake; remove towel. Beat jam or preserves to soften, and spread over cake. Roll and sprinkle with powdered sugar.

Chocolate Delight Cake

½ cup butter
½ cup sugar
2 eggs
1¾ cups cake flour
½ cup cocoa powder

1 teaspoon baking soda
¼ teaspoon cinnamon
¼ teaspoon salt
1 cup milk
1 teaspoon vanilla

Preheat oven to 350 degrees. Cream together butter and sugar until light and fluffy. Add eggs, beating after each addition. Sift together flour, cocoa powder, baking soda, cinnamon, and salt. Add half of the flour mixture to the egg mixture. Add milk and vanilla, then stir in remaining flour mixture. Bake for 25 to 30 minutes in a greased 9x11-inch baking pan.

Festive Fig Cake

2 cups flour
1 teaspoon salt
1 teaspoon baking soda
1½ cups sugar
1 cup oil

3 eggs
1 cup buttermilk
1 cup fig preserves
1 teaspoon vanilla
½ cup chopped nuts

In a mixing bowl, combine flour, salt, soda, and sugar. Add oil and eggs. Slowly add milk and preserves. Blend well, adding vanilla and nuts. Pour into greased and floured Bundt pan. Bake at 325 degrees for 45 minutes.

Tea Cakes

1 cup butter
2 cups sugar
3 eggs, slightly beaten
4 cups flour

2 teaspoons baking powder
1 teaspoon vanilla
¼ teaspoon cinnamon
⅛ teaspoon salt

Cream butter and sugar. Add eggs, flour, baking powder, vanilla, cinnamon, and salt. Roll on floured board and cut. Sprinkle with sugar, and bake at 400 degrees for 12 to 15 minutes.

Christmas Pudding

Butter
4 eggs, beaten
¼ teaspoon salt
¾ cup sugar
2 teaspoons vanilla
1½ teaspoons grated
   lemon peel

3 cups whole milk
1½ cups cooked rice
½ cup seedless raisins
Topping (recipe follows)

In a buttered 2-quart casserole dish, combine eggs, salt, sugar, vanilla, and lemon peel. Combine milk and rice. Stir into egg mixture, and then stir in raisins. Set casserole in a pan of hot water. Bake uncovered at 300 degrees for 1½ to 2 hours. After first 30 minutes, insert spoon at edge of pudding and stir from bottom. Continue baking until knife inserted in the middle of pudding comes out clean.

Topping:
2 teaspoons sugar
1 teaspoon cinnamon

Mix sugar with cinnamon. Sprinkle over cooked pudding. Brown quickly under the broiler. Serve hot or cold. Makes 6 to 8 servings.

Lemon Curd Topping

6 large lemons
2 cups sugar
1½ sticks unsalted butter,
   cut into 12 pieces

Water
6 eggs, room temperature,
   slightly beaten

Remove yellow part of peel from lemons, using vegetable peeler. Chop finely in a food processor. Squeeze lemons to measure 1 cup of juice. Heat juice with peel, sugar, and butter in double boiler over simmering water until sugar dissolves and butter melts. Strain eggs into lemon mixture. Cook, stirring constantly, about 20 minutes. Do not boil! Pour into a bowl, and place plastic wrap on surface to prevent skin from forming; let cool. Cover and refrigerate overnight before using. This old-fashioned custard is also wonderful on scones or with fresh fruit.

Oatmeal Pie

2 beaten eggs
⅔ cup regular oatmeal, cooked
⅔ cup light corn syrup
⅔ cup sugar
¼ teaspoon salt

1¼ teaspoons vanilla
½ cup melted butter
1 (9 inch) unbaked pie shell
Whipped cream (optional)
Dash nutmeg (optional)

Combine eggs with oatmeal, syrup, sugar, salt, and vanilla. Add butter and mix thoroughly. Pour into pie shell. Bake for 1 hour at 350 degrees. Let cool before serving. Serve with whipped cream sprinkled with a dash of nutmeg.

Walnut Spice Cake

2 cups flour
1¼ teaspoons baking soda
1 teaspoon ground ginger
1 teaspoon ground cinnamon
½ teaspoon freshly ground pepper
½ teaspoon salt
1 egg
½ cup sugar

1 stick butter, melted and cooled
¼ teaspoon grated lemon peel
¾ cup hot water
⅓ cup molasses
⅓ cup honey
¾ cup chopped walnuts
Lemon Curd Topping
  (see p. 86)

Preheat oven to 350 degrees. Grease and flour an 8-inch square baking dish. Sift first 6 ingredients together. Whisk egg and sugar in a large bowl to blend. Whisk in butter and lemon peel. Combine hot water, molasses, and honey in a large cup. Add to butter mixture alternately with dry ingredients, beginning and ending with dry ingredients. Mix in walnuts. Transfer to prepared dish. Bake until springs to touch, about 50 minutes. Cool cake for 5 to 10 minutes on rack. Cut cake into squares. Serve warm or at room temperature, spooning Lemon Curd Topping over each piece.

Pineapple Upside-Down Cake

3 (8 ounce) cans sliced
  pineapple in heavy syrup
¼ cup butter
¾ cup light brown sugar
½ cup pecan halves
1 cup all-purpose flour
¾ cup sugar

1½ teaspoons baking powder
½ teaspoon salt
¼ cup shortening
½ cup milk
1 egg
Whipped cream

Drain pineapple slices, reserving 2 tablespoons of syrup. In a 10-inch iron skillet with heat-resistant handles, melt butter over medium heat. Add brown sugar, stirring until sugar is melted. Remove from heat. Arrange 8 pineapple slices on sugar mixture. Put one pineapple slice in the center. Fill centers with pecan halves. Halve 3 more pineapple slices. Arrange around inside edge of skillet, and fill with pecans. Set aside. Sift flour with sugar, baking powder, and salt in a large bowl. Add shortening and milk. Beat for 2 minutes or until mixture is smooth. Add egg and reserved 2 tablespoons pineapple syrup; beat 2 minutes longer. Gently pour cake batter over pineapple in skillet, spreading evenly, being careful not to disturb pineapple. On rack in center of oven, bake 40 to 45 minutes at 350 degrees or until golden in color and surface of cake springs back when pressed with fingertip. Let skillet stand on wire rack 5 minutes to cool just slightly. With spatula, loosen cake from edge of skillet, and turn upside down; shake gently. Lift from skillet. Serve cake warm with whipped cream.

Custard Pie

4 eggs, slightly beaten
½ cup sugar
1 teaspoon vanilla
½ teaspoon almond extract
¼ teaspoon salt

2½ cups whole milk, scalded
1 (9 inch) unbaked pie shell,
   chilled
Nutmeg

Combine eggs, sugar, vanilla, almond extract, and salt. Blend well. Gradually add milk, stirring constantly. Pour filling into pie shell. Bake pie for 25 to 30 minutes in a 400-degree oven or until knife inserted halfway between center and outside comes out clean. Remove baked pie to cooling rack; sprinkle with nutmeg. Cool custard pie completely before cutting.

Frosted Pecan Cake

½ cup shortening
¾ cup sugar
½ cup brown sugar
2 eggs
2⅛ cups cake flour
2 teaspoons baking powder

½ teaspoon salt
¾ cup whole milk
1 teaspoon vanilla extract
1 cup chopped pecans
Pecan Frosting (recipe follows)

Combine shortening and sugars; cream well. Beat in eggs. Sift cake flour, baking powder, and salt. Add alternately with milk. Add vanilla. Fold in chopped pecans. Pour batter into two 8-inch round pans. Bake in 350-degree oven for 25 to 30 minutes. Top with frosting (see p. 94).

Pecan Frosting

2 cups powdered sugar
3 tablespoons butter
1¼ teaspoons vanilla
Pinch salt

1 tablespoon caramel syrup
5 tablespoons or more water
1 cup chopped pecans

Beat all ingredients except pecans. Spread on cooled cake. Put chopped pecans between layers of cake and on top.

Egg Custard Pie

4 eggs, beaten
2¼ cups milk
2 tablespoons butter
1 cup sugar

2 tablespoons flour
1 teaspoon vanilla
1 (9 inch) unbaked pie shell
Nutmeg

Mix all ingredients and beat well. Put into pie shell. Bake in preheated 450-degree oven for 10 minutes; reduce heat to 350 degrees, and bake 40 to 50 minutes more. Sprinkle with nutmeg. Bake pie on a cookie sheet.

Aunt Jo's Brownies

2 eggs
1 cup granulated sugar
½ teaspoon salt
1 teaspoon vanilla
⅓ cup shortening, melted

2 ounces unsweetened
  chocolate squares, melted
¾ cup flour
1 cup chopped walnuts

Beat eggs lightly with spoon. Stir in sugar, salt, and vanilla. Add shortening and chocolate. Stir in flour and walnuts. Spread mixture into a greased 8-inch square pan. Bake at 325 degrees for about 30 minutes.

Cream Cheese Bars

1 stick butter or margarine
1 box golden yellow cake mix
1 pound powdered sugar

2 eggs
8 ounces cream cheese

Mix butter and cake mix until crumbly. Spread in a greased 9x13-inch pan. Cream powdered sugar, eggs, and cream cheese. Spread over cake mix crust. Bake at 350 degrees for 35 minutes.

Frosty's Fruitcake

⅓ cup butter
1 cup sugar
2 eggs
1 teaspoon vanilla
1 cup whole milk

2 cups bread flour
3 teaspoons baking powder
¼ teaspoon salt
Fruit Filling and Icing
 (recipe follows)

Cream butter and sugar well. Add yolks of eggs and vanilla; mix well. Add milk. Sift together flour, baking powder, and salt. Add to mixture. Mix in beaten egg whites. Bake in 3 greased and floured 9x11-inch pans in oven at 375 degrees for about 20 minutes. Cool for 15 minutes, and then remove from pan.

Fruit Filling and Icing:

2½ cups granulated sugar
¾ cup boiling water
1 teaspoon baking powder
2 egg whites

1 teaspoon lemon juice
1 cup each figs, cherries,
   and pineapple, all finely cut

Boil sugar, water, and baking powder without stirring until syrup spins a thread. Beat egg whites until dry; add syrup gradually, beating constantly until right consistency to spread. Add flavoring and cool. Add fruit to ⅓ of this icing, and spread thickly between layers of the cake. Cover top and sides of cake with remaining plain icing.

Nanny's Fancy Cheesecake

Crust:

20 graham crackers

2 teaspoons sugar

¼ cup butter, melted

Preheat oven to 325 degrees. Roll crackers with rolling pin to make fine crumbs. Place crumbs in springform pan, and stir in sugar. Add butter and mix well. Press crumbs against sides and around bottom of pan to form crust. Bake crust for 7 minutes. Remove from oven and let cool.

Filling:

3 eggs

18 ounces cream cheese, softened

1½ cups sugar

⅛ teaspoon vanilla

1½ pints sour cream

3 tablespoons sugar

1 teaspoon vanilla

2 pints fresh strawberries
   or blueberries

3 tablespoons currant jelly

Separate eggs. Place egg yolks, cream cheese, 1½ cups sugar, and ⅛ teaspoon vanilla in mixing bowl. Beat with mixer until light. In a separate bowl, beat egg whites to stiff peaks. Gently mix ¼ of these egg whites into cream cheese mixture to lighten. Fold in remaining egg whites. Fill crust with cream cheese mixture, and smooth very lightly. Place in oven, and bake at 350 degrees for 30 to 45 minutes until cheesecake is set. A toothpick inserted near edge should come out clean, and center should barely move when cake is moved back and forth lightly. Remove and cool, leaving the oven on. In mixing bowl, place sour cream with remaining sugar and vanilla. Blend well. Lightly spoon this mixture over cheesecake, and return to oven for additional 20 minutes. Remove from oven, cool, and refrigerate. Remove from pan, and place on a decorative plate. Arrange fruit on top. Place jelly in small pan, and melt on top of stove. Using pastry brush, paint top of fruit with melted jelly to glaze, and refrigerate until needed.

Snowflake Cake

½ cup butter
½ cup sugar
½ teaspoon lemon juice
¼ cup whole milk
5 egg whites, beaten to a stiff froth

2 cups pastry flour
½ teaspoon baking soda
1 teaspoon cream of tartar
Snowflake Frosting
(see p. 103)

Cream butter and sugar. Add lemon juice, and beat until light and fluffy. Add milk and egg whites. Combine flour, baking soda, and cream of tartar. Add to mixture and mix well. Bake in 350-degree oven for 25 to 30 minutes. Top with frosting.

Snowflake Frosting

3 egg whites
2 cups powdered sugar

½ cup coconut
½ teaspoon lemon juice

Beat egg whites to a stiff froth. Add powdered sugar gradually, then add coconut and lemon juice. Mix lightly.

Plum Pudding

1 pound stale bread
1 pint hot milk
½ pound sugar
8 egg yolks, beaten just until creamy
1 pound raisins, stoned and floured
1 pound currants, washed and floured
¼ pound citron, cut in strips
  and dredged with flour

1 pound beef suet,
  chopped fine and salted
½ cup wine
½ cup brandy
1 tablespoon each nutmeg,
  mace, cinnamon, and cloves
8 egg whites, beaten to a stiff
  froth
Plum Pudding Sauce (see p. 106)

Soak bread in milk, and let it stand and cool. When cold, add sugar and egg yolks. Add raisins, currants, citron, beef suet, wine, brandy, and spices. Beat well together. Add egg whites last. Pour into a cloth, previously scalded and dredged with flour; tie it firmly, leaving room for the pudding to swell. Boil for 6 hours. Serve with sauce. It is best to prepare the ingredients the day before serving and cover closely to keep a skin from forming.

Plum Pudding Sauce

1 cup sugar
½ cup butter
4 egg yolks, well beaten

½ cup brandy
Pinch salt
1 cup whole milk

Cream together sugar and butter. When light and creamy, add egg yolks. Stir in brandy, salt, and milk. Beat this mixture well, and place it in a saucepan over medium heat. Stir it until it cooks sufficiently to thicken like cream. Do not let boil. Serve warm over plum pudding.

Christmas Cookies & Bars

For to us a child is born, to us a son is given,
and the government will be on his shoulders. And he
will be called Wonderful Counselor, Mighty God,
Everlasting Father, Prince of Peace.

ISAIAH 9:6 NIV

Walnut Balls

1 cup butter
⅓ cup brown sugar
1 teaspoon vanilla
2 cups flour

½ teaspoon salt
1½ cups finely chopped
  walnuts
Powdered sugar

In a mixing bowl, cream butter, sugar, and vanilla until fluffy. Sift flour and salt together; add to creamed mixture. Mix well. Stir in walnuts. Shape dough into 1-inch balls. Bake on ungreased cookie sheet for 12 to 15 minutes at 375 degrees. Remove from cookie sheet. Roll in powdered sugar while still warm.

Gingersnaps

1½ cups shortening
2 cups sugar
2 eggs
½ cup molasses
4 cups sifted flour

2 teaspoons baking soda
2 teaspoons cinnamon
2 teaspoons cloves
2 teaspoons ginger
Sugar

Cream shortening and sugar; beat in eggs, then add molasses. Sift together flour, baking soda, and spices. Add sifted ingredients to shortening and mix well. Roll mixture into 1-inch balls. Roll balls in sugar, and place 2 inches apart on slightly greased cookie sheet. Bake at 375 degrees for 12 to 15 minutes. Cool slightly before removing from cookie sheet.

Butter Cookies

3 cups flour
1 teaspoon baking powder
½ teaspoon salt
1 cup butter
¾ cup sugar

1 egg
2 tablespoons sour cream
1½ teaspoons vanilla
Decorative sugars

Mix flour, baking powder, and salt. Set aside. Cream butter and sugar. Add egg, sour cream, and vanilla. Blend in dry ingredients. Roll in decorative sugars and cut. Bake at 400 degrees for 5 to 8 minutes.

Spice Bars

1 cup raisins
½ cup oil
1 cup hot water
1 cup sugar
1½ teaspoons cinnamon
½ teaspoon allspice
¼ teaspoon cloves

1 teaspoon nutmeg
1 egg, slightly beaten
1¾ cups flour
¼ teaspoon salt
½ cup nuts, chopped
1 teaspoon baking soda

Bring raisins, oil, and water to a boil. Allow to cool. Add sugar, cinnamon, allspice, cloves, nutmeg, egg, flour, salt, nuts, and baking soda. Mix well. Place in a greased 9x13-inch pan, and bake for 20 minutes at 375 degrees.

Oatmeal Cookies

1 cup raisins
1 cup water
¾ cup shortening
1½ cups sugar
2 eggs
1 teaspoon vanilla
2½ cups flour

½ teaspoon baking powder
1 teaspoon salt
1 teaspoon baking soda
1 teaspoon cinnamon
½ teaspoon cloves
2 cups rolled oats
¼ cup chopped nuts

In a medium saucepan, simmer raisins and water over low heat until raisins are plump, about 20 to 30 minutes. Drain raisin liquid into measuring cup, adding enough water to make ½ cup. Cream shortening, sugar, eggs, and vanilla. Stir in raisin liquid. Sift together flour, baking powder, salt, baking soda, and spices, and add to mixture. Add rolled oats, nuts, and raisins. Drop by rounded teaspoonfuls 2 inches apart onto ungreased baking sheet, and bake for 8 to 10 minutes at 400 degrees.

Jolly Raspberry Bars

1 cup butter
1 cup packed brown sugar
1½ cups flour
½ teaspoon baking soda
½ teaspoon vanilla

1½ cups old-fashioned oats,
    uncooked
1 (10 ounce) jar red raspberry
    preserves
¼ cup sliced almonds, toasted

Cream butter and sugar. Add flour and baking soda; mix well. Blend in vanilla. Stir in oats. Spread mixture onto bottom of greased 9x13-inch baking pan; spread with preserves to within ½ inch of outer edge of pan. Sprinkle with almonds. Bake at 375 degrees for 22 to 25 minutes. Cool and cut into bars.

Momma's Molasses Cookies

¾ cup butter
1 cup sugar
¼ cup dark molasses
1 egg
2 cups flour
2 teaspoons baking soda

½ teaspoon vanilla
1 teaspoon cinnamon
½ teaspoon cloves
½ teaspoon ginger
½ teaspoon salt

Combine butter with sugar. Add molasses and egg. Add remaining ingredients except flour. Beat for 30 seconds. Stir in flour, and beat for 1 minute. Drop by tablespoonfuls onto cookie sheets, and bake for 10 to 12 minutes at 375 degrees until edges begin to brown lightly. Let cool and store in airtight tins.

Sugar Cookies

½ cup butter, softened
1 cup sugar
1 egg, unbeaten

1½ teaspoons vanilla
½ cup buttermilk
3¼ cups self-rising flour
Sugar

Sift flour. In a large mixing bowl, combine butter, sugar, egg, and vanilla. Beat until mixed well. Add buttermilk and flour gradually. Roll out on well-floured surface to ¼-inch thickness. Sprinkle with sugar, roll in lightly. Cut with floured Christmas cookie cutters. Place on greased cookie sheet. Bake at 375 degrees for 10 to 12 minutes.

Sour Cream Cookies

¼ cup shortening
¼ cup butter, softened
1 cup sugar
1 egg
1 teaspoon vanilla
2⅔ cups flour

1 teaspoon baking powder
½ teaspoon baking soda
½ teaspoon salt
¼ teaspoon nutmeg
½ cup sour cream

In a mixing bowl, cream shortening, butter, sugar, egg, and vanilla. Add flour, baking powder, baking soda, salt, and nutmeg. Gradually add sour cream. Mix well. Roll ¼ inch thick; sprinkle with sugar, and cut with floured cutter. Bake 8 to 10 minutes at 425 degrees.

Me-ma's Chocolate Chip Cookies

1⅛ cups sifted flour
¼ teaspoon baking soda
½ teaspoon salt
½ cup shortening
¼ cup brown sugar
½ cup granulated sugar

1 egg, beaten
1½ teaspoons vanilla
8 ounces semisweet chocolate
  bits
½ cup walnuts, if desired

Sift flour, baking soda, and salt together. Set aside. In a mixing bowl, cream shortening and sugars. Add egg and vanilla. Mix thoroughly. Add sifted ingredients. Fold in chocolate bits and walnuts. Drop from teaspoon onto greased baking sheet. Bake in 350-degree oven for 8 to 10 minutes.

Maple Sugar Cookies

1 cup shortening
1 cup sugar
1 cup maple syrup
2¾ cups flour
2 teaspoons ginger
½ teaspoon cloves

1 teaspoon salt
4 teaspoons baking soda
1½ teaspoons cinnamon
¼ teaspoon nutmeg
1 cup buttermilk

In a mixing bowl, cream shortening and sugar. Add maple syrup. Sift 2 cups flour with other dry ingredients, and add alternately to first mixture with the buttermilk. Add enough of the remaining flour to make a soft dough. Roll and cut into shapes. Sprinkle sugar on top, and bake 5 to 8 minutes at 400 degrees.

Refrigerator Cookies

1 cup packed brown sugar
1 cup butter, melted
1 egg
3 cups flour

1 teaspoon cinnamon
½ teaspoon baking soda
½ teaspoon salt
1 cup chopped nuts, if desired

In a mixing bowl, combine brown sugar and melted butter. Beat in egg. Add dry ingredients. Roll into a long roll, and wrap in waxed paper. Refrigerate overnight. Remove waxed paper and slice. Bake at 375 degrees for 6 to 8 minutes.

Pa's Peanut Butter Cookies

2½ cups flour
1 teaspoon baking powder
1 teaspoon baking soda
¼ teaspoon salt
1 cup butter

1 cup peanut butter
1 cup sugar
1 cup brown sugar
2 eggs
1 teaspoon vanilla

Stir together first 4 ingredients and set aside. Beat butter and peanut butter until smooth. Beat in sugars, eggs, and vanilla. Add flour mixture. If necessary, chill dough. Shape in 1-inch balls, and bake on ungreased cookie sheet at 350 degrees for 12 minutes.

Ma's Banana Cookies

1 cup sugar
½ cup sour cream
1 cup butter

2 eggs
1 cup mashed bananas
½ teaspoon salt

2 teaspoons baking powder
1 teaspoon baking soda
4 cups flour

Mix all ingredients. Bake at 350 degrees for 12 to 15 minutes.

Frosting:
½ cup butter
1 (8 ounce) package cream cheese

1 pound powdered sugar
1 teaspoon vanilla

Cream ingredients in order listed, and sprinkle with holiday decorations.

Great-Grandma's Raisin-Filled Cookies

1 egg
1 cup sugar
½ cup shortening
1 teaspoon vanilla
1 teaspoon baking soda

½ teaspoon salt
2 teaspoons baking powder
3½ cups flour
½ cup milk

In a mixing bowl, cream egg, sugar, shortening, and vanilla. Sift together baking soda, salt, baking powder, and flour. Add to creamed mixture alternately with milk. On floured surface, roll out dough, and cut into circles with a round cookie cutter. Place half of the circles on an ungreased baking sheet, then make filling.

Filling:

1 cup raisins

1 cup nuts

2 tablespoons cornstarch

½ cup sugar

½ cup water

1 tablespoon butter

Combine filling ingredients in a saucepan over medium heat. Bring to a boil, and let sit until cool. Put filling on top of cutouts, and top with remaining cutouts. Seal the edges so that the filling does not leak out. Bake for 10 to 12 minutes at 350 degrees.

Great Pumpkin Cookies

4 cups flour
2 cups old-fashioned oats,
    uncooked
2 teaspoons baking soda
2 teaspoons ground cinnamon
1 teaspoon salt
1½ cups butter, softened
2 cups firmly packed brown sugar
1 cup granulated sugar

1 egg
1½ teaspoons vanilla
1 (16 ounce) can pumpkin
1 cup semisweet chocolate
    chips
Icing
Sprinkles or other cookie
    decorations

Combine flour, oats, baking soda, cinnamon, and salt; set aside. Cream butter and sugars. Beat until light and fluffy. Add egg and vanilla; mix well. Add pumpkin alternately with dry ingredients. Mix well. Stir in chocolate chips. For each cookie, drop ¼-cup dough onto lightly greased cookie sheet. Spread into a pumpkin shape using a thin metal spatula or the back of a large metal spoon. Add a bit more dough to form a stem. Bake at 350 degrees for 20 to 25 minutes, until cookies are firm and lightly browned. Remove and cool on racks. Decorate using your favorite icing and candies. Makes about 32 large cookies.

Breads, Muffins
& Other Edible Gifts

"Glory to God in the highest, and on earth
peace to men on whom his favor rests."

LUKE 2:14 NIV

Gingerbread

2¼ cups flour
1 cup dark molasses
½ cup shortening
1 teaspoon baking soda
1¼ teaspoons cinnamon

⅓ cup sugar
¾ cup hot water
1 egg
1 teaspoon ginger
¾ teaspoon salt

Mix all ingredients in large mixing bowl. Pour into greased 9-inch square pan. Bake at 325 degrees for 50 minutes. Serve warm with whipped cream.

Chocolate Shortbread

1 cup butter, softened
¾ cup powdered sugar
1½ cups flour
Pinch salt

⅓ cup cocoa
Walnuts, halved
Maraschino cherries

Preheat oven to 300 degrees. Cream butter and powdered sugar until fluffy. Stir in flour, salt, and cocoa. Mix well. If too soft, chill in refrigerator for ½ hour. Shape into 1-inch balls, and place on an ungreased cookie sheet about 2 inches apart. Flatten balls with a fork. Top with walnut half or cherry. Bake for 20 to 25 minutes. Remove from oven, and let cool slightly before removing from pan.

Christmas Date Nut Loaf

2 eggs, room temperature
½ cup sugar
1 teaspoon vanilla
2 teaspoons baking powder

1 cup flour
¼ teaspoon salt
½ pound dates, finely chopped
½ pound chopped pecans

Separate egg whites from yolks. Beat egg yolks until light and fluffy. Add sugar slowly. Add vanilla. Sift together baking powder, flour, and salt, and gradually add to mixture. Beat well. Add dry ingredients, including dates and pecans, to egg yolk mixture. In a separate bowl, beat egg whites until stiff but not dry. Fold egg whites gently into mixture. Bake at 325 degrees for 60 minutes or until done.

Nana's Banana Bread

1 cup sugar
⅓ cup butter or vegetable
    shortening
2 eggs, beaten
3 small overly ripened
    bananas, mashed
2½ cups flour, divided

1 teaspoon baking soda
6 tablespoons buttermilk
1 teaspoon vanilla
1 teaspoon lemon juice
Pinch salt
Chopped nuts, optional

In a mixing bowl, cream together sugar and butter. Add eggs and bananas. Add
1 cup flour. Stir baking soda into buttermilk and add to mixture. Add remaining
flour, vanilla, lemon juice, and salt. Grease and flour 1 large bread pan. Bake at
350 degrees for 45 minutes to 1 hour, testing with toothpick for doneness. Cool
about 5 minutes, and remove from pans to rack. If desired, chopped nuts may be
added before baking.

Christmas Sweet Bread

1 cup butter
1 cup sugar
1 cup sorghum syrup
⅛ teaspoon baking soda

3 teaspoons baking powder
¼ teaspoon salt
3 cups flour
4 eggs, beaten

Melt butter in a saucepan. Add sugar and syrup. Heat until lukewarm. In a separate bowl, mix baking soda, baking powder, and salt with flour. Add to first mixture. Add well-beaten eggs and mix thoroughly. Pour into well-greased bread pan, and bake at 275 degrees 18 to 20 minutes or until done.

Honey Wheat Bread

1½ cups water
1 cup cream-style cottage cheese
½ cup honey
¼ cup butter
6 cups flour
1 egg

1 cup whole wheat flour
2 tablespoons sugar
2 teaspoons salt
2 packages active dry yeast
Shortening
Extra butter

Heat water, cottage cheese, honey, and butter in a medium saucepan until very warm but not boiling. In a large bowl, combine 2 cups of leveled flour with warm mixture. Add egg, whole wheat flour, sugar, salt, and yeast. Beat for 2 minutes. By hand, stir in remaining flour to make a stiff dough. Knead dough on well-floured surface until smooth and elastic (about 2 minutes). Place in greased bowl. Cover; let rise in warm place until light and doubled in size (45 to 60 minutes). Grease two loaf pans with shortening. Punch down dough; divide and shape into 2 loaves. Place in greased pans. Cover; let rise in warm place until doubled in size. Heat oven to 350 degrees. Bake 40 to 50 minutes until deep golden brown and loaves sound hollow when tapped. Immediately remove from pans. Brush with butter.

Cinnamon Raisin Bread

½ cup milk
½ cup sugar
1½ teaspoons salt
¼ cup butter
2 packages dry yeast

½ cup hot water
2 eggs, beaten
5 cups flour
2 cups raisins
Cinnamon

In a large saucepan, scald the milk. Add sugar, salt, and butter. Mix well. Cool to lukewarm. In a separate bowl or cup, dissolve the yeast in water. Combine yeast with milk mixture. Add eggs and 3 cups flour; beat well. Beat in raisins. Gradually add flour to make moderately firm dough. Knead on lightly floured board about 5 minutes until dough is smooth and elastic and does not stick to hands. Grease surface very lightly; let rise in warm place until double in size, about 1 hour. Punch dough down; knead lightly once again, then divide in half. Roll each half into rectangle about 9 inches wide. Sprinkle with cinnamon and roll up, laying seam side down in greased 9x5-inch loaf pan. Let rise again until double in size, about 40 minutes. Bake in 400-degree oven for about 50 minutes.

Apple Bread

2 medium apples, peeled,
  coarsely grated
2 tablespoons lemon juice
3 cups flour
1½ teaspoons baking soda
1 teaspoon salt
2½ teaspoons pumpkin pie spice

¾ cup shortening
1¼ cups packed brown sugar
3 eggs, room temperature
1½ teaspoons vanilla
¾ cup strong tea, room
  temperature
½ cup chopped nuts

Mix grated apples with lemon juice and set aside. Combine flour, baking soda, salt, and spice; mix thoroughly and set aside. Cream shortening and sugar. Add eggs, one at a time, beating well after each addition. Stir in apples and vanilla. Stir in flour mixture alternating with tea. Stir in nuts with last addition of dry ingredients. Pour into 2 greased 8x4-inch loaf pans. Bake in 350-degree oven for 1 hour or until done. Let stand 5 minutes; remove from pans, and cool on wire rack.

Pumpkin Bread

3 cups sugar
3½ cups flour
2 teaspoons baking soda
½ teaspoon salt
1 teaspoon cinnamon

1 teaspoon ginger
1 cup oil
4 eggs, beaten
⅔ cup water
1 (16 ounce) can pumpkin

Sift sugar, flour, baking soda, salt, and spices into large mixing bowl. Make a well in center of the dry ingredients. Add oil, eggs, water, and pumpkin. Blend well; pour into two small greased loaf pans. Bake at 325 degrees for 1 hour and 10 minutes.

Old-Time Holiday Bread

2 cups whole milk
⅓ cup sugar
1 tablespoon salt
1 stick butter
1 rounded tablespoon
  shortening

⅓ cup warm water
1 teaspoon sugar
3 packages dry yeast
6½ cups flour or more
5 eggs, well beaten, divided
1½ cups raisins

In a saucepan, heat milk, sugar, salt, butter, and shortening. Cool slightly until no longer hot. In a separate bowl, add water and sugar. Sprinkle yeast into water and sugar, and let it rise until bubbly, about 10 minutes. Add just enough flour to make a thick dough, and let rise for 10 to 15 minutes. Sift 6 cups flour into another large bowl. Add milk mixture, 4 eggs, and yeast mixture; add up to 1 more cup flour if dough is too sticky. Work by hand with up and down motion about 15 minutes, until dough is fairly smooth and shiny. Place in bowl, sprinkle with flour, and cover bowl with aluminum foil until it rises for about 2 hours. After bread has risen, divide into 3 parts. Take each piece, and pull it to about a 10-inch circle. Sprinkle with raisins. Roll up and shape into a rope about 10 inches, making 3 ropes out of each ball. Braid and put into a well-greased pan. Brush top with remaining beaten egg. Bake at 350 degrees for 30 to 40 minutes or until brown. Cool on racks.

Christmas Pound Cake

1 pound butter
2 cup sugar
4 cups flour
12 eggs
2 teaspoons vanilla

1½ teaspoons lemon extract
½ teaspoon salt
½ teaspoon nutmeg
1 cup sour cream

Cream butter and sugar. Slowly add flour and eggs. Add remaining ingredients and mix well. Bake for 1 hour at 325 degrees. Bake at 350 degrees for another 15 minutes. Cool completely. Wrap in foil, and tie with a festive ribbon.

Pumpkin Ginger Muffins

1½ cups canned pumpkin
5 tablespoons applesauce,
  room temperature
2 egg whites, whipped
½ cup apple juice, room temperature
2 cups packed brown sugar
1½ cups flour

2 teaspoons baking soda
2 teaspoons baking powder
1 teaspoon salt
4 teaspoons ginger
1 teaspoon nutmeg
¼ cup sugar mixed with
  1 tablespoon cinnamon

Grease and flour muffin pans. In a mixing bowl, combine pumpkin, applesauce, whipped egg whites, and juice. In a separate bowl, combine sugar, flour, baking soda, baking powder, salt, ginger, and nutmeg. Mix wet ingredients with dry ingredients just until moistened. Fill muffin tins ⅔ full. Bake for 25 minutes at 350 degrees. Sprinkle with cinnamon sugar as soon as taking out of the oven, if you wish.

Holiday Muffins

½ cup vegetable oil
3 eggs
¼ cup brown sugar
2 teaspoons vanilla
1 carrot, peeled and grated
1 apple, peeled and grated
½ cup golden raisins
½ cup shredded coconut
1 cup flour

½ cup old-fashioned rolled oats
¼ cup wheat germ
½ cup chopped walnuts
1 teaspoon baking soda
1 teaspoon ginger
½ teaspoon baking powder
¼ teaspoon salt
Dash nutmeg

In a mixing bowl, beat together oil, eggs, sugar, and vanilla until well blended. Add remaining ingredients. Mix on medium speed until all ingredients are blended. Do not overmix. Divide batter into greased muffin tins, filling them to the top of each cup. Bake about 20 minutes in a 375-degree oven.

Peppermint Christmas Candy

1 pound sugar
½ pint cold water

6 drops peppermint oil
Red and green food coloring

In a large saucepan, mix together sugar and cold water until sugar is dissolved. Add peppermint oil, and cook for five minutes. Remove from heat, and stir a little until mixture becomes cloudy. Add food coloring; pour immediately (before granules start to form) into small candy molds, or drop quickly on lightly buttered paper from a teaspoon. This candy must be poured quickly, or granules will form.

Pecan Puffs

1 cup butter, softened
2 tablespoons brown sugar
2 tablespoons sugar
1 teaspoon vanilla

2 cups flour
1 cup chopped pecans
Powdered sugar

Preheat oven to 300 degrees. Cream butter and sugars. Beat until fluffy. Stir in vanilla. Add flour and stir until combined. Mix in chopped pecans. Roll into small balls, and place on an ungreased cookie sheet. Bake for 15 minutes or until bottoms are golden brown. While still hot, roll each cookie in powdered sugar to coat, and set on a rack to cool.

Sugared Pecans

1 egg white
1½ teaspoons water
½ teaspoon salt

1 teaspoon cinnamon
¾ cup sugar
½ pound pecan halves

Preheat oven to 300 degrees. With fork, beat egg white and water. Set aside. Combine salt, cinnamon, and sugar in a resealable plastic bag. Place pecans in egg mixture. Remove with slotted spoon to drain off excess moisture. Place in bag and shake. Line a baking pan with foil, and bake pecans for 30 to 45 minutes, stirring every 15 minutes. Freeze in an airtight container. (These will keep for up to two months.)

Potato Candy

1 medium potato, baked
3 cups powdered sugar

¼ teaspoon vanilla
2 cups peanut butter

Remove insides of potato, and mash with a fork while still hot. Add powdered sugar and vanilla until mixture is the consistency of pie dough. Roll it between two pieces of waxed paper until about ¼ inch thick. Remove top sheet of waxed paper. Spread peanut butter over entire surface of dough. Roll dough into a log, and wrap it in the bottom sheet of waxed paper. Place on a hard surface in the refrigerator until firm. Peel off waxed paper. Slice and enjoy.

Peanut Brittle

2 cups sugar
1 cup light corn syrup
½ cup water
1 cup butter

2½ cups dry roasted peanuts,
    unsalted and warmed
1 teaspoon baking soda
1 teaspoon vanilla

In a large saucepan over medium heat, combine sugar, corn syrup, and water. Stir until sugar dissolves. When syrup comes to a boil, blend in butter and stir frequently. Continue cooking until candy thermometer registers 280 degrees. Immediately add peanuts, and stir constantly until thermometer reaches 305 degrees. Remove from heat, and quickly add baking soda and vanilla, mixing well. Immediately pour into 2 jelly roll pans, and spread as closely as possible to edges. When cool, lift from pans, using spatula, and break into pieces.

Date Candy

2 cups sugar
1 cup whole milk
1 cup chopped dates

1 teaspoon vanilla
2 tablespoons butter
1½ cups nuts

Cook sugar, milk, and dates over low heat until a drop of the mixture forms a soft ball in a small amount of cold water. Remove from heat, and add vanilla, butter, and nuts. Beat until mixture begins to get cool and hard. Pour into a wet towel in a long roll. Roll up and put in refrigerator. When set up and completely cold, slice in ¼-inch pieces and wrap in waxed paper.

Festive Fudge

3 cups sugar
⅔ cup cocoa
Dash salt
1½ cups evaporated milk

4½ tablespoons butter
1 teaspoon vanilla
1 cup chopped walnuts

In a large saucepan, blend sugar, cocoa, and salt until all lumps are dissolved. Gradually add evaporated milk and mix well. Place over medium heat and stir often. Let mixture boil up to the top of the pan and back down. Remove from heat. Add butter and vanilla. Mix well. Add nuts. Beat fudge as it cools until it thickens and loses its gloss. Quickly spread into a buttered 9-inch pan. Let cool. Cut into squares before completely cooled.

Pull Taffy

2 cups molasses
1 cup brown sugar
2 tablespoons butter

⅓ cup water
1 tablespoon vinegar
Pinch baking soda

Boil all ingredients together. Taffy is done when a few drops in cold water become brittle. Pour into a buttered dish, and allow to cool. When cool enough to handle, rub butter on hands; pull small portions at a time until taffy is light in color. Cut in small pieces, and wrap in waxed paper.

Popcorn Balls

3 cups popping corn
1½ cups molasses

1 cup sugar
1 tablespoon baking soda

Pop 3 batches of popping corn. Place in large pan. In a saucepan, bring molasses and sugar to a boil. While boiling, stir in baking soda. Pour over popcorn and mix. Allow to cool. Slightly grease hands, and shape into balls. Wrap in waxed paper, and tie with ribbons.

Apple Butter

2 dozen medium apples
2 quarts sweet cider
3 cups sugar

1½ teaspoons cinnamon
½ teaspoon cloves

Wash and quarter apples. Cook apples in cider until tender. Press through a sieve or food mill. Measure 3 quarts apple pulp. Cook pulp until thick. As the pulp thickens, stir frequently to prevent sticking. Add sugar and spices. Cook slowly until thick, about 1 hour, stirring frequently. Pour into hot jars, leaving ¼-inch headspace. Seal and process in simmering water bath for 10 minutes. Makes 5 pints of apple butter.

Chow Chow for Christmas

3 jalapeno peppers
1 quart bell peppers, chopped
1 quart green tomatoes, ground
1 quart cabbage, ground

1 quart onion, chopped
1 quart sugar
1 quart vinegar
5 tablespoons salt

Grind jalapeno peppers with bell peppers. Put all ingredients in a large pot. Let mixture boil until it changes color and onions are transparent. Put in hot sterilized jars and seal, following lid directions. Tie jars with a red ribbon, and give in gift baskets at Christmastime.

INDEX